IEA

Institute of Economic Affairs
1989

First published in September 1989
by
THE INSTITUTE OF ECONOMIC AFFAIRS
2 Lord North Street, Westminster, London SW1P 3LB

Occasional Paper 82

ISSN 0073-909X

ISBN 0-255 36223-4

Printed in Great Britain by
GORON PRO-PRINT CO LTD, LANCING, WEST SUSSEX

Set in Berthold Plantin 11 on 13 point

Contents

Foreword

THIS *Occasional Paper* reproduces the second IEA Special Lecture delivered by the Governor of the Bank of England at the Queen Elizabeth II Conference Centre on 26 July 1989. In the Lecture the Governor gives his views on the nature and prospects of European monetary reform and integration. Given Britain's present reluctance to enter the European Monetary Union and the fear in some quarters that proposals for a central bank and a common currency will restrict competition and overly centralise decision-making, the Governor's views will be of great interest to all students of economic policy.

As is now customary with Special Lectures we have invited Professor Patrick Minford of Liverpool University and a Senior Research Fellow at the IEA, to comment on the Governor's analysis and underlying assumptions. Professor Minford, one of the foremost monetary economists in the UK, responds to the Governor's lecture with characteristic forthrightness and rigour. His commentary adds a challenging counterweight to the views of a professional banker who must work in the world in which ideas are tempered by politics and compromise.

The IEA dissociates itself from the views of its authors. We reproduce the text of Mr Leigh-Pemberton's Lecture together with Professor Minford's commentary as a contribution to the debate over European economic and monetary reform and eventual integration. The Institute of Economic Affairs gratefully acknowledges the generosity of British Airways, which, for the second year, has sponsored the IEA's Special Lecture.

September 1989 CENTO VELJANOVSKI

The Authors

RT HON ROBIN LEIGH-PEMBERTON was born in Kent in January 1927. He was educated at St Peter's Court School, Broadstairs, and Eton College. After military service with the Grenadier Guards he read classics at Trinity College, Oxford, where he is now an Honorary Fellow.

Mr Leigh-Pemberton was called to the Bar in 1954 and practised in London and on the South East circuit until 1960. He is an Honorary Master of the Bench of the Inner Temple. Subsequently he became a director of Birmid-Qualcast Ltd. (Chairman, 1975-77), Redland Ltd. and the Equitable Life Assurance Society. He joined the board of the National Westminster Bank in 1972, becoming Deputy Chairman in 1974 and Chairman in 1977, a position he held until he was appointed Governor of the Bank of England for a five-year term from 1 July 1983. He has subsequently been reappointed for a further five years.

Mr Leigh-Pemberton has been a member of the National Economic Development Council since 1982 and is a Fellow of the Chartered Institute of Bankers and the Royal Society of Arts. He is a Liveryman of the Mercers Company.

From 1963 to 1977 he was a member of Kent County Council, being Chairman of the Council from 1972 to 1975. He was Pro-Chancellor of the University of Kent at Canterbury from 1977 to 1983, when an honorary Doctorate of Civil Law was conferred on him. After serving as Vice Lord Lieutenant for 10 years, he succeeded Lord Astor as Lord Lieutenant of Kent in August 1982. Mr Leigh-Pemberton was appointed to the Privy Council in 1987.

He is married and he and his wife Rose have five sons.

A. P. L. (PATRICK) MINFORD has been Edward Gonner Professor of Applied Economics, University of Liverpool, since 1976, and is a Senior Research Fellow at the IEA. Formerly Visiting Hallsworth

Research Fellow, University of Manchester, 1974-75. Sometime Consultant to the Ministry of Overseas Development, Ministry of Finance (Malawi), Courtaulds, Treasury, British Embassy (Washington); Editor of *National Institute Economic Review*, 1975-76.

Professor Minford is the author of *Substitution Effects, Speculation and Exchange Rate Stability* (1978), and of essays published in *Inflation in Open Economies* (1976); *The Effects of Exchange Adjustments* (1977); *On How to Cope with Britain's Trade Position* (1977); *Contemporary Economic Analysis* (1978); co-author of *Unemployment: Cause and Cure* (1983, 2nd edn. 1985). He has been a member of the IEA's Advisory Council since 1985. He contributed papers to two IEA Seminars: 'Macro-economic Controls on Government', in *The Taming of Government* (IEA Readings 21, 1979), and 'Monetarism, Inflation and Economic Policy', in *Is Monetarism Enough?* (IEA Readings 24, 1980). He also contributed 'Restore Market Momentum and Fight On' to *Could Do Better* (Occasional Paper 62, 1982), and 'From Macro to Micro via Rational Expectations' to *The Unfinished Agenda* (1986); he was joint author (with Michael Peel and Paul Ashton) of *The Housing Morass* (Hobart Paperback No. 25, 1987); and editor of *Monetarism and Macro-economics* (IEA Readings 26, 1987).

The Future of Monetary Arrangements in Europe

The Rt. Hon. ROBIN LEIGH-PEMBERTON

IT IS A GREAT PRIVILEGE to have been asked to give the second of the Institute of Economic Affairs's annual lectures. The inaugural Lecture given last year by the Chancellor of the Exchequer set a demanding standard and established the IEA Lecture as a major event in the calendar. I think this makes it incumbent on me to address a topical and important issue. Bearing in mind the IEA's record of confronting controversial and complex subjects, I have chosen an issue that is also emotive: the future of monetary arrangements in Europe. And if anyone doubts that this is emotive, may I remind you that members of the Commons Treasury Committee have already accused me of High Treason on account of my participation in the Delors Committee work.

Economic and monetary union does unquestionably raise some very important issues relating to economic and political sovereignty, such as the degree of control member-states would continue to have over economic, and especially monetary, policy and also whether the UK would have to give up sterling as part of a European move to a single currency. It is therefore essential that there should be a full and rigorous public debate and that a detached view should be taken of the various issues and arguments that have been raised. I hope I can do that in this Lecture.

EMU: The Delors Committee Report

Perhaps I should start by recalling that the objective of Economic and Monetary Union (or so-called EMU) is not new. While the Treaty of Rome speaks only of '. . . an ever closer union', the progressive realisation of EMU was first agreed by the

Hague Conference in 1969 and was confirmed by all the member-states of an enlarged Community in Paris in 1972. The objective was further reaffirmed by the Single European Act of 1985, and last year, recalling this long-standing commitment, the Hanover European Council set up the Delors Committee to analyse the concrete stages needed to reach economic and monetary union.

But while the commitment is longstanding, what would be involved is not generally understood. Indeed, one of the problems that has loomed largest over the past few months has been with definitions. I should therefore make clear my own definitions. I shall take full 'monetary union' to mean a single currency area that requires an area-wide monetary policy, and 'economic union' to be an unrestricted common market with some co-ordination of policies between its regions. EMU therefore covers both.

Delors's Three Stages

The Delors Committee envisaged a three-stage approach to achieving EMU. In Stage 1, greater convergence of economic performance would be brought about by strengthening policy co-ordination and completion of the internal market through the 1992 project. It has already been agreed that, as part of that process, the remaining controls on capital flows will be abolished, in most cases by 1990, creating a single financial area in which capital, as well as goods and labour, will be able to move freely. Before the end of Stage 1 – for which incidentally the Committee did not set a time-scale – all Community currencies would under the Delors proposals participate on the same terms in the Exchange Rate Mechanism (ERM) of the European Monetary System (EMS).

In Stage 2, the transition would begin from the co-ordination of independent national monetary policies to the formulation and implementation of a common monetary policy. Exchange rate realignments within the ERM framework would not be ruled out, but there would be a growing preference for other adjustment mechanisms. As part of this process, there would be increasing co-ordination of official foreign exchange operations involving non-member currencies, leading eventually to a common Community approach.

In Stage 3, exchange rates would be locked irrevocably and ultimately a single European currency could replace national currencies. This would require the transition to a single monetary policy to be completed.

Institutional Changes

The Delors Committee also envisaged that, in its later stages, this process would be accompanied by institutional changes. In Stage 1, the existing framework for economic and monetary policy co-ordination would be strengthened and, in particular, there would be enhanced policy surveillance by the Council of Economic and Finance Ministers and by the Committee of Central Bank Governors. In Stage 2, a new institution, which the Delors Group called the 'European System of Central Banks' (ESCB), would be set up that would progressively assume the responsibility for monetary policy scheduled for Stage 3. And in Stage 3 itself, when the ESCB became responsible for a Community-wide monetary policy, the Community institutions would assume an increased role in the process of international policy co-operation with non-Community countries.

This, then, was the Delors Committee's outline for concrete stages leading to full EMU. I should stress that the Committee did *not* address whether EMU was desirable or recommend a timetable for achieving it. Indeed, it would have been quite wrong to ask a group of technicians an essentially political question. The decisions falling to politicians must, however, depend heavily on an assessment of the technical *economic* factors which will determine both the feasibility and desirability of a transition to EMU. I want to consider those economic factors in some detail.

Optimum Currency Areas

In doing so, it is important to be clear about the circumstances in which Stage 3 of the Delors outline could be obtained. I will therefore begin with a rather abstract but nevertheless fundamental question: Under what conditions would full monetary union with a common currency be desirable or, put another way, in what circumstances would the benefits of a single currency exceed the costs?

The benefits are fairly easy to identify. Where prices within an area are quoted in a common currency, uncertainties arising from unpredictable exchange rate fluctuations within the area are removed. In consequence, business decisions are not complicated by a need to take account of possible exchange rate changes within the currency area, which would help to improve confidence, particularly in relation to investment decisions with long time horizons. Furthermore, there would no longer be any transactions costs associated with exchanging one currency for another or with trying to hedge against changes in rates.

These benefits stem from reducing the costs of exchanging goods and services. Larger gains will therefore be available, the greater the extent of trade and investment between the regions of a currency area. The cost reductions are, moreover, themselves likely to encourage trade and lead to a more efficient allocation of resources within the area.

The potential drawbacks of monetary union are rather more complex and difficult to assess. The main costs arise from the loss of autonomy over domestic monetary policy and, in particular, the loss of nominal exchange rate variations as a means of promoting economic adjustment. The ability to realign is most valuable where the local currency prices of capital and labour within a region are inflexible and where labour is relatively immobile. In those circumstances, exchange rates can have an important effect on a region's competitiveness, at least in the short run, and can thus help to cushion the region against shocks which affect it more adversely than its trading partners. If, on the other hand, a region trades extensively with its neighbours, its wages are likely to respond to a rise in import prices following a fall in the exchange rate, while shocks with distinctive effects are less likely if its economy is structurally similar to those of its partners.

Economic and Cultural Integration the Key

The question of how the benefits and costs of monetary union compare as regards Europe therefore relates to the degree of economic and cultural integration. Our everyday perceptions are not necessarily reliable in this respect. Indeed, attitudes towards integration within the Community vary greatly, and it is surely legitimate that there should be a range of opinions on the big issues raised by EMU. But, for better or worse, as a technical matter, Europe is gradually evolving in a direction in which the benefits of a common currency are becoming larger and the economic costs are diminishing. As regards the volume of trade and the mobility of factors of production, the Community has moved some considerable way to meeting the conditions for an optimal currency area. Since the late 1950s, intra-European trade has grown rapidly – both in absolute terms and relative to the total trade flows of the member-states. For each of the major Community economies – France, Germany, Italy and the UK – visible trade with other Community members accounts for around 50 per cent of total trade and is around 10 per cent of national product.

The establishment of the single internal market through the 1992 programme will further increase the pace of economic integration in the Community by enhancing the mobility of both labour and capital. But the Community is, and will plainly continue to be, less integrated than a successful industrialised single currency area like the United States, where the benefits of having a common currency surely outweigh the costs. For example, US trade is more integrated and labour mobility, which depends in part on cultural factors and not least a common language, is much higher than in Europe. Cultural differences – and therefore the institutional and structural differences which reflect them – will continue to limit economic integration in the Community, however much they enrich the Community in a broader sense.

If economic and monetary union in Europe is desired, other measures will therefore undoubtedly be required. In broad terms, one could envisage a range of approaches. At one extreme there would be what one might call the 'activist strategy', which would involve moving rapidly towards monetary union as a means of speeding up the process of economic integration but which would raise some important regional policy issues. At the other extreme lies the minimalist position of making steps towards monetary union totally dependent upon increased integration. In between there are strategies which in varying degrees would make movement towards monetary union dependent upon increased economic and cultural integration, but would also recognise that active moves towards greater monetary union would actually enhance economic integration.

Transition to EMU – Alternative Strategies

(a) *An Activist Strategy*

As I have indicated, the activist strategy would use steps towards monetary union to force the pace of *economic* integration. There would accordingly be a timetable for narrowing the Exchange Rate Mechanism bands, locking exchange rates and establishing a centralised institutional framework. Deadlines for the ultimate introduction of a single currency and monetary policy could also be set. At an early stage, exchange rate movements would cease to be a means of economic adjustment, which would instead have to rely on changes in relative prices, productivity and levels of economic activity.

The effects of this activist strategy cannot be known with certainty. It might in principle accelerate economic integration, for example if lower exchange rate volatility led to increased trade flows. But it could also have the effect of accentuating pressures towards regional divergence – or, put another way, could mean that some regions would be relatively disadvantaged by monetary union. Long-standing structural problems could be aggravated as there would be a risk that real wages would tend to converge more rapidly than levels of productivity might justify. This risk would be greater if, as well as requiring centralised macro-economic policies, the activist EMU blueprint was linked to policies emphasising Community-wide standards of, for instance, incomes and welfare benefits. In these conditions, monetary union could have the perverse effect of increasing unemployment problems in lower productivity regions.

Whatever the immediate response to such regional problems – supporting the extra unemployed, subsidising wages or providing cheap capital to create employment at increased wage levels – large fiscal transfers would result, which would tend to reduce the market incentives for lasting adjustments and could create tensions within the Community. More generally, a balance would have to be struck in seeking to mitigate the effects of shocks on regions without unduly delaying economic integration by slowing the rate at which factor mobility increased.

(b) *Exchange Rate Adjustment as a Response to Regional Problems?*

If rapidly implemented monetary union could aggravate the difficulties of the Community's less prosperous regions, the question arises as to whether they should be compensated for losing recourse to currency depreciation as an adjustment mechanism.

In my view, however, currency devaluation is not a remedy for relative poverty. It does not conjure resources into existence and, as we in this country know all too well, in the long run it is at best neutral in its real effects, while at worst it can increase the costs of reducing inflationary pressures.

Exchange rate adjustment can, on the other hand, play a short-term role in national responses to transient or unexpected shocks which may affect countries differently. It is not, however, a necessary instrument even in these circumstances. Indeed, it is important not to forget that similar problems of regional disparities can arise within a single country or currency area where exchange rate adjustment is impossible. This is well illustrated in the United States by the difficulties the oil-producing state of Texas has experienced over the past few years. I am not aware, however, of any suggestion that Texas should try to solve its problems by breaking away from the dollar (and creating a separate Texan currency). Nor has there been much explicit federal aid for Texas. What does exist in the USA – though to a lesser extent than in other industrialised countries – is an automatic mechanism for stabilising income, through progressive federal taxation and social security arrangements. Such mechanisms can temper the effects of unexpected shocks on the people living in particular regions and reduce the pain of the adjustments that would be necessary if such shocks proved to be persistent.

An adherent of the activist strategy might therefore argue not only that EMU required some form of Community-wide progressive tax and welfare scheme, but also that it should be introduced sooner rather than later in order to reduce the risks of aggravating regional problems. As I have already indicated, however, it would be vital that any such scheme did not embody a uniform level of social benefits across the Community, as that would be likely to exacerbate unemployment in areas where labour was less productive.

Moreover, I suspect the main issue is political. While the existing member-states are sufficiently politically and culturally cohesive to employ redistributive welfare programmes that go some way to alleviate regional problems, it is not at all clear that the citizens and nations of the Community are ready to see redistributive mechanisms on the scale that would be necessary to address Community regional problems. The level of the fiscal transfers required might therefore become a source of divisiveness within the Community.

In summary, therefore, the activist approach would be liable to create or exacerbate regional disparities that could probably not be solved satisfactorily in economic terms or acceptably in political terms.

(c) *Evolutionary Strategies*

I have dealt at length with the first, activist strategy and highlighted the regional policy issues that it would raise. The evolutionary strategies that I identified earlier would be very different in their effects, as movement towards a currency union would not be allowed to get ahead of developments in economic and cultural integration and progress towards the optimum conditions for a single currency area. Rather, constitutional and institutional change would occur only when the growing links between Community economies created a need for them.

An evolutionary strategy would not, however, necessarily be passive. It would include the steps described in Stage 1 of the Delors Report, and in particular the establishment of the single European market, which will be tremendously important in bringing about economic integration. But monetary arrangements will also have an influence upon the pace of integration.

An intermediate strategy would therefore be to aim for *parallel* progress towards the twin objectives of economic integration and monetary union. It is not easy to judge what the rate of progress along the path to EMU would be under this approach or to identify the institutional arrangements which would be needed at particular points on that path. In contrast with the activist strategy but in common with the minimalist approach, the development of Community-wide policy-making structures would depend on economic and social conditions.

Fiscal Policy and EMU

Under all of the strategies for moving to EMU, greater co-ordination of economic policy between national authorities would be desirable. But there is a very important question as to how far and fast such co-ordination should go and, more particularly, to what extent it should cover co-ordination of fiscal policy. This has perhaps so far been the most controversial issue raised by the Delors Report as it bears directly on matters of political sovereignty, including the right of national governments to tax and spend.

The Delors Committee argued that EMU would need to be accompanied by limitations on national fiscal policy and, specifically, on the size of budget deficits. The Committee believed that, without any such limitation, the governments of individual member countries might not be subjected to effective discipline. Financial markets would provide the most natural channel for applying this discipline, but it must be recognised that they have a patchy record in assessing sovereign risks, and might well assume that member-states would not, in the final analysis, be allowed to default. In other words, there is a possibility that they would act on the basis that there was an implicit collective guarantee of individual member-states' debts.

If market discipline on borrowing was inadequate, individual nations would be able to borrow on a scale liable to have a significant macro-economic effect on the Community as a whole. At worst, this could lead to extremely disorderly situations and at the very least it could affect the level of interest rates in the area as a whole. Adjustment would therefore be required in the Community's aggregate monetary and fiscal policy. Just as there is currently a need for co-ordination between monetary and fiscal policy within individual countries, there would need to be co-ordination of European-wide monetary and aggregate fiscal policy in an economic and monetary union.

Gold Standard and US as Role Models?

Against this, it can in principle be argued that the example of the Gold Standard and the arrangements in the USA for the fiscal policy of individual states show that, in fact, no limitations on national fiscal policy would be needed in a monetary union. There are some problems with this argument, however.

First, the Gold Standard was, as its name implies, a commodity standard. As such, the system did not need a single central bank to control its supply and (provided there were no major discoveries causing a rapid rise in the stock of gold) ruled out persistent inflation, including that which might otherwise have been generated by fiscal policies. In addition, so long as the tie to gold held, governments did not have the option of inflating away their debt. As a result, budget deficits were not considered prudent, at least in peacetime, either by national governments or financial markets and, in consequence, the issue of whether or not to set limits on the size of deficits did not arise.

Secondly, the fiscal history of the American states is not so clear-cut. Some did run deficits in the mid-19th century. Indeed, some states ran up large debts and defaulted, suffering the capital market consequences. It was against this background and the diminishing prestige of the states following the Civil War that it was found expedient to amend states' constitutions, restricting their powers to borrow either at all or in excess of capital spending programmes. The US example does not therefore suggest a painless route to federal fiscal soundness.

On balance, it therefore seems to me that there could well be risks in ruling out some form of fiscal policy co-ordination. I should immediately stress, however, that very careful consideration needs to be given to the *form* of co-ordination that would be appropriate in an economic and monetary union in the European Community. Certainly I cannot see that constraints on member-states' fiscal positions would need to be particularly tight. Rather their purpose might only be to prevent major deviations from generally agreed fiscal policy. Most decisions, including the tax structure and the scale and nature of government expenditure, would remain the preserve of member-states, and the impact on sovereignty need not in practice therefore be material for member-countries choosing to adopt a prudent fiscal stance.

Conclusions on Transition Strategies to EMU

I have discussed a range of strategies for approaching economic and monetary union. My own conclusion is that there are real and serious risks in forcing the pace towards EMU by establishing an activist, centralised policy-making structure ahead of progress on economic integration. Moreover, I believe the alternative, evolutionary strategies have advantages. It would be harder to predict how fast we would progress and what kind of union we would end up with, but in my view that need not be a disadvantage.

And here I should make one thing absolutely clear: one cannot say of the road to economic and monetary union described in the Delors Report that taking the first step requires one to be able to predict with confidence that full EMU will be reached. As I indicated earlier, the Delors Report set out a number of major steps which would represent a significant move towards a more fully-integrated Community. Each step should be taken only when it is seen as having a balance of beneficial consequences. In this sense, if further steps were to prove impossible or undesirable, each stage would be a better resting place than the preceding one.

The all-or-nothing claims made about starting on the road to economic and monetary union are therefore misleading. Nor does the Delors Report make any such claims. The decision to take the steps contained in Stage 1 of the Committee's outline was, to quote the report, 'a decision to embark on the entire process'. There is no implication that embarking on the process should require one to plough on even if progress beyond some point would plainly be unwise. The Madrid Summit recognised how undesirable such a rigid strategy would be.

Indeed, if the kind of monetary union set out in the Delors Report were rejected, for example on the ground that it entailed an undesirable surrender of national powers, then looser forms of monetary union might be sought. For example, one alternative would involve the removal of all barriers to trade and the free movement of capital, services and labour – that is, the creation of the internal market – and the establishment of fixed, but ultimately still adjustable, exchange rates. This form of union – which may be termed 'soft union' – would in fact be similar in many ways to what is envisaged for the end of Stage 2 of the Delors Report's outline. It would not be monetary union in a strong sense, but one could describe it as a point on a spectrum – and it need not be only a temporary stopping point.

A number of such alternatives are potentially available and deserve consideration, and in this connection it is noteworthy that the Madrid European Council identified the Delors Report as providing one possible blueprint for EMU but not necessarily the only one. Work on Stages 2 and 3 therefore continues.

But we should not let different views about the desirability of remoter objectives or the means of achieving them divert attention from the present task of completing the first steps towards greater integration. All member-countries are fully committed to the completion of the internal market, where the goal is the free movement of goods and services, labour and capital between all member-states. As I have already said, this in itself will do much to increase European economic integration. Much more can be done on the co-ordination of both fiscal and monetary policy and on the creation of a Community-wide competition policy aimed at strengthening market mechanisms. There is, I believe, no disagreement between member-states on the desirability of progress on all these fronts, and certainly no reluctance on the part of the British Government. Indeed, faster progress can be made by concentrating on those initial steps towards which all are genuinely committed rather than by dragging those who are as yet unpersuaded into areas where they are reluctant to go.

ERM – The Issue of UK Participation

For the United Kingdom, one of the most important elements of the Madrid Summit agreement on Stage 1 was that there will be full participation in the Exchange Rate Mechanism of the European Monetary System on the same terms for all members – that is to say, within the narrow band.

Since ERM membership is not always adequately distinguished from EMU, I think I should stress in this connection that the issues raised by sterling membership of the ERM are of a different order of magnitude from those involved in economic and monetary union, whether soft or hard. In particular, ERM membership would not require any significant institutional changes because, as a member of the Community, we already participate in the Committee of Central Bank Governors and the European Monetary Co-operation Fund. Indeed, in practice there would be no greater transfer of sovereignty than occurred through our membership of the IMF during periods of fixed exchange rates.

Furthermore, while entry into the Exchange Rate Mechanism would have effects that lie largely within the realm of experience, moves towards economic and monetary union would, in the words of the Delors Committee, 'represent a quantum jump' towards a system at whose final form we can only guess.

What Gains from ERM Membership?

What, then, would we stand to gain from ERM membership? There is a range of potential benefits. Our participation should, for example, visibly confirm our commitment to greater European economic integration and, it is widely believed, would therefore enhance our influence within the Community, both in the debate on EMU and more generally. By the same token, there is a real risk that, if we were to remain outside the ERM and were to abstain from the EMU debate, our influence within the Community could diminish. It is partly in this context that one hears concerns expressed about the dangers of a two-speed Europe and potential damage to London's position as the pre-eminent European financial centre. While these latter dangers can certainly be exaggerated, it would be unwise to be complacent about London's future at a time when the competitive pressures in the financial services industry globally are already so intense.

But there are also potential *economic* benefits available from the ERM. First, there is a good deal of evidence that the system has, especially in recent years, brought its members a significant reduction in intra-EC exchange rate volatility, which would of course be valuable for UK business. Furthermore, this increased currency stability has not, in their circumstances, been at the expense of more volatile interest rates. I should add in this connection, however, that ERM membership will not lessen the impact of volatility against non-Community currencies. Nor will it do anything to reduce that volatility. There will continue to be a considerable volume of trade with non-Community countries and also very large capital flows between Community and non-Community countries. As now, fluctuations in the value of other currencies – particularly the US dollar – caused by events outside Europe will continue to have major implications for policy-makers in the Community.

Improved Inflation Control?

A second possible economic benefit relates directly to the control of inflation. It is clear that some ERM member-countries have dramatically improved their inflation performance in recent years. While the same has been true of the UK outside the ERM, one of the potential benefits of our membership is that it could provide an additional anchor for prices. The experience of France and Italy is particularly relevant in this respect. They have used the link to the Deutschemark which the Exchange Rate Mechanism has provided to help reduce their inflation rates towards the German level. This has not been costless and both countries have, in the short run, lost some competitiveness which will have affected trade and activity. But the benefit is equally undeniable. Since the early 1980s the inflation gap with Germany has been much reduced in Italy and virtually eliminated in France. Certainly the authorities in these countries doubt whether this could have been achieved, at least at a comparable adjustment cost, without the discipline of ERM membership.

In this connection, it is sometimes argued that the commitment implied by ERM membership to maintain the external value of one's currency could strengthen the credibility of the authorities' counter-inflationary policy. In its strongest form, this argument holds that inflationary expectations could be sufficiently reduced so that the parties to wage bargains would be induced to settle for lower increases and inflation would fall quickly and sharply, allowing monetary policy to be less tight.

This seems rather optimistic to me. Indeed, it is important to recognise that none of the potential economic advantages that I have identified would accrue painlessly or automatically, simply as a consequence of ERM membership. They have to be worked for through disciplined policy actions, whether inside or outside the exchange rate framework. Membership would be no panacea. If the exchange rate commitment were to be credible, it would need to be absolutely and unequivocally clear that policy would be continuously directed to the counter-inflationary discipline required to sustain it.

Risks and Strains of the ERM

It is also important to recognise that joining the ERM would not be riskless. UK participation could create strains on the mechanism and it is relevant in this respect that sterling is more heavily traded than any of the ERM currencies apart from the Deutschemark. The depth and liquidity of the sterling money and asset markets generate such a weight of mobile funds that a shift in confidence would be likely to cause greater flows into or out of sterling than is the case for the other non-Deutschemark, ERM currencies.

The UK economy also has some important structural differences from other Community economies, the most notable being the continued, albeit diminished, importance of oil to our trade position. Capital markets in the future may, as they have at times in the past, respond to changes in the price of oil by putting pressure on exchange rates and it may not be easy to offset these by interest rate changes which are consistent with domestic monetary objectives. Moreover, the UK's direct investment outside the Community is larger than that of our Community partners. Developments in third currencies and markets will therefore tend to have different effects on sterling than on other ERM currencies.

Of course, every new entrant to the ERM since its inception has been a potential source of strain, and in this sense UK participation would not be unique. It remains to be seen how serious the strains would be, and what measures, if any, would be needed to overcome them. But it is fair to say that the importance of our distinguishing structural features has been declining and will most likely continue to do so.

ERM – The Timing of UK Entry

This leaves the particularly vexed, if also well-worn, question of the timing of our entry into the ERM. In many respects, the arguments here parallel those relating to the appropriate pace of progress on monetary union itself. Just as there are risks in forcing the pace on monetary union, so early entry into the ERM designed to force the pace of financial convergence with our Community partners – most importantly in inflation – could carry risks. The question is whether conjunctural convergence – that is, a convergence in the cyclical, rather than structural, position of the economy – should have gone further before our entry or whether membership could itself be used as a means to bring about faster convergence.

My own judgement is clear. It would be a mistake to enter the mechanism in circumstances where our anti-inflationary policy might be compromised or undermined. This could happen if we wished to keep interest rates high for domestic reasons but, by committing ourselves to too low a parity, for example, we were pushed towards lowering interest rates to keep sterling within its band. It would therefore be unwise to enter the mechanism with the UK economy significantly out of balance with the other major member-countries.

In those circumstances, there could be no assurance that we would enter at an approximately appropriate rate, and it has to be remembered that too low a rate would have damaging implications for inflation, just as too high a rate could have severe effects on activity and investment. It would be an inauspicious start if we had to seek a realignment shortly after joining the system, and even worse if in the longer run sterling's presence in the system became a recurrent source of pressure for realignment. Spain's experience of joining in not wholly dissimilar circumstances will be illuminating.

One could attempt to avoid an early conflict between the Government's domestic economic aims and the domestic monetary implications of commitment to the ERM by entering with a sufficiently wide band. But the cost of such flexibility would be to risk reducing – or even undermining – the potential advantages of exchange rate stability and discipline.

So the problem is not easily solved. Ultimately, we can enter the mechanism only at the prevailing market rate and we cannot know within a wide range whether that rate would be capable of being sustained without significant disturbance to domestic economic conditions.

At present there is a difference in the cyclical position of the UK economy relative to the major member-countries. There are significant differences in the rates of inflation and both real and nominal interest rates are several percentage points apart. Adjustment is in train, but there is still some way to go. We could be more confident in choosing the time, and therefore the rate, at which to enter the ERM when there are greater signs of convergence in demand conditions and inflation performance between the UK and our major Community partners.

As the adjustment in the UK takes its course – and as the expected narrowing of the structural differences between the UK and other Community countries takes place – the risks involved in our entry to ERM will decrease. Meanwhile, the transition to a single internal market will also be nearer completion and the remaining capital controls will be being dismantled, taking us closer to the conditions necessary for UK membership *and* making it more desirable.

Conclusions

The two issues I have addressed in this Lecture – EMU and ERM – relate to *very different* time-horizons. The pace at which monetary union in Europe is approached should partly depend upon the pace of economic and cultural evolution. This cannot be expected to happen dramatically in a few years, and in my view the establishment of a single currency area in Europe therefore remains distant. But important steps towards EMU will nevertheless be taken over the next few years.

For the UK, one of these steps – our entry into the ERM – has a number of large potential advantages, although it is important not to expect miracles. In contrast to EMU's requirement for progress towards economic and structural integration, ERM entry depends (more particularly) on conjunctural convergence over a much shorter timespan than the period which fundamental integration will require.

I believe that our efforts should now be focussed on attaining these initial steps and that European visionaries, as well as pragmatists, can unite in this aim.

Commentary: The Governor Breaks Euro-Silence

by

PATRICK MINFORD

WHEN THE Governor of the Bank of England, Mr Robin Leigh-Pemberton, gave his Institute of Economic Affairs lecture, he was able to use the occasion to break his silence on the infamous Delors Report on European Monetary Union, which he had signed. The lecture therefore gave him the chance to justify himself before an audience most of whom rated Monsieur Delors's credentials for market liberalism at about the same level as Beelzebub's for the taking of confessions.

His lecture divided into two parts: a long-term look at the question of European Monetary Union (EMU) and a short-term discussion of whether and when Britain should join the European Monetary System (EMS) as a full member participating in the Exchange Rate Mechanism (ERM). Let me take these in the same order as the Governor did, starting with EMU.

The Long Term: European Monetary Union?

The Governor's plea was that European Monetary Union is a necessary part of the long-term framework for a frontier-free market. But the achievement of that Union must proceed in stages, beginning with the post-Madrid EMS, so that mistakes can be made and learnt from.

On the later stages, involving in Stage Two fiscal co-ordination and larger regional transfers, and in Stage Three the creation of a Europe-wide central bank, the Leigh-Pemberton view is just what you would expect from a central banker. Democratic governments get away with murder in the deficits they run, borrowing against the collateral of the taxes of future generations, or even appealing to an implicit guarantee from their fellow union members. Unelected central bankers are by contrast a sober, responsible lot who can exercise a useful restraining hand. Regional transfers are the necessary sweetener for this discipline and the inability to devalue. Finally, a European central bank would eventually bring this discipline to its apotheosis.

To be fair to the Governor, he distances himself from the headier parts of Delors, repeatedly warning of the possible political and regional difficulties if the pace of monetary union is forced. He backs the Madrid formula for the UK to join the full EMS and effectively suggests trial-and-error from then on, leaving the Vision to take its chance.

As well he might. For who would control such a central bank? Why should independent governments not make rational choices about how much to borrow on open markets, smoothing the burden of taxation across the fluctuating requirements of public spending? Why should regional transfers be passed by successful regions to regions which will not adjust their wages and prices? Is this not inviting poor productivity and excessive wages in a series of Ruhrs, Southern Italys and Northern Englands? Has not the UK experience since 1979 shown how well 'declining' regions can do if exposed to market forces?

And so on and on (see 'Nitpicking' below). The Delors Report is a monstrous conspiracy of centralism, mounted by an *ad hoc* alliance of central bankers and bureaucrats whose interests wonderfully coincide in this assault on consumer choice and democratic rights. But let us choke back our indignation and ask, as Mrs Thatcher did after Madrid, for a clear alternative.

Suppose the EMS becomes a reformed system without capital controls and with genuine free competition across the financial sectors of Europe. Post-Madrid each country must keep its exchange rate within a narrow band around its parity; the parity can be changed only *in extremis.*

The reason for such rigidity is that under free capital movements any country operating a policy of readily adjustable 'fixed' parities will be swamped by speculative attack from the vast reservoir of mobile capital. Only exchange controls can sustain a régime, like the present EMS, so precariously placed midway between fixity and floating.

How Would the New EMS Work?

Though there will be exchange intervention and support for the rates, each central bank remains independent and acts as a check on the excesses of the others.

Imagine that the rates have been fixed between the major currencies for a few years, and that inflation in each of them has been in a low range of, say, below 3 per cent.

Now one currency becomes more inflationary. Consumers and firms switch their holdings out of it, freely and easily with controls abolished. Its central bank loses reserves in possibly vast amounts, others gain them. The process must stop quickly, and the inflationary tendency is arrested.

But there is an important and desirable asymmetry. If one currency becomes less inflationary than the others, people switch into it, and its central bank gains reserves in large amounts, whilst others lose them. The central bank is likely to put up with this for longer than they, so they will move to match the lower inflation.

So inflation is pushed downwards by this competition. No central bank can exploit its consumers or firms through an inflation, essentially because they can freely switch to other currencies.

It turns out that the abolition of controls – *all* controls, including implicit ones through credit allocations and restricted financial competition – is enough to change the EMS fundamentally. It is at present a bureaucratic mess in which intervention and controls permit countries both to hold their exchange rates and pursue incompatible monetary policies. It is scheduled to become an engine for low inflation and monetary competition.

The moral is plain: Stage One is enough. It will lead by its own natural momentum to low inflation and a monetary union of independent central banks policing each other through competition.

Mrs Thatcher's Whitehall committees will no doubt come up

with lots of complicated schemes for The Alternative to Delors. She should ignore them all in favour of what already Herr Pohl, the head of the Bundesbank, has hinted at and what the Governor too is basically saying: that a reformed EMS would be a true evolutionary alternative.

'Nitpicking' the Governor's Logic

In his discussion of EMU, Mr Leigh-Pemberton develops a view of how a common currency area works which is highly questionable. In my account above I glossed over these technical issues in order to focus on the main policy matters. However, it was to some degree the same intellectual errors that inspired the Delors Report.

The Governor argues that regional adjustment is hampered by a common currency. His idea is that if a region suffers a loss of demand for its products, say, requiring a fall in real wages, this would be more easily achieved via devaluation than by a fall in wages relative to prices. But we now know from the experience of many devaluations that it is no easier to change real wages that way than by transparent wage and price movements; basically if real wages will not fall transparently because of supply-side rigidities, then no amount of devaluation will make them fall either.

Of course, there might be some effect of devaluation in the short term, but that is another matter; any gain is at least partly balanced by the inflationary effect. The point here is that there is no long-run loss which needs to be compensated by regional transfers.

On the regional issue the Governor does make the valuable point that producing a common level of welfare benefits across the EEC would truly create regional problems, since high benefits in low-wage areas would generate unemployment and dependency. But this has no necessary connection with monetary union.

On fiscal policy the Governor argues that somehow an 'irresponsible' government, borrowing much, could raise interest rate risk premia for the rest of the EEC. But this presupposes some sort of inter-government guarantee or some correlation of other governments' actions with this government's. Nothing of this sort is assumed by the Delors Report or anyone else in the debate; it implies a degree of economic union that goes well beyond anything so far contemplated.

It is true that as one economy expands with high borrowing, it will raise the risk-free real interest rate at home. But this does not imply that real interest rates in the rest of the EEC must rise too; though nominal interest rates are equalised, the same is not true of real rates nor are real exchange rates immutable. Consumers and producers elsewhere are as free as under floating rates to reach optimal voluntary exchanges. The only difference is in monetary transmission.

There is no intellectual justification for a regional or fiscal co-ordination aspect to EMU. EMU is a purely monetary proposal. People have attempted to link other aspects to EMU coat-tails but that is just political opportunism. The Governor has too much truck with this position, even though he comes out right in the end on policy.

Britain and the EMS: When Will the Time Be Ripe?

The Governor's remarks would hardly have been complete without a section on the vexed short-term question of when and if Britain should join the full EMS.

Given the above description of a reformed, competitive-currency EMS, no monetarist could really argue with it. For essentially it would mean that our citizens could choose the lowest inflation currency in Europe for their transactions. If the Bank and the Treasury could not restrain their inflationary desires, the competitive discipline would soon force them to.

The main objections to the current EMS are that because countries can quite easily move parities, exchange controls are necessary (thus shifting and disguising the instability still created by divergent monetary policy) and long periods of over- and under-valuation are sustained to reconcile 'fixed' parities with divergent monetary policy. The reformed EMS would remove these, creating both a free capital market and a quasi-constitutional bulwark against inflationary policies.

Thus, if it happens, the Governor, like all monetarists, must welcome such a system and regard it as fit for Britain to join.

The question left is one of timing. The conditions laid down by Mrs Thatcher in Madrid were, first, that there should be genuine freedom from capital market controls – in other words, it would truly be a reformed system – and, second, that Britain should have got its inflation down, essentially to the German rate.

The Governor supports this formula. He argues that to use joining the EMS as a *mechanism* for getting our inflation rate down would be foolhardy. It would get in the way of the tight monetary policy required to do the job, because interest rates would be held down by the EMS. We would in effect get a repeat of what happened in early 1988 when in trying to shadow the Deutschemark we pushed interest rates down to 7 per cent to stop the pound rising through 3.00 DM; and we all know where that has led us subsequently.

The Governor is right. As he says, there is no magic way of getting inflation down; it has to be done by monetary sweat and toil, tight money first enforced relentlessly then coming to be expected to happen indefinitely. Counter-inflationary credibility, as he puts it, has 'to be worked for through disciplined policy actions' 'continuously directed to' counter-inflation. A period of low interest rates, of 6 per cent or so, produced by capital market arbitrage between Frankfurt and London, on the back of an EMS short-term commitment to hold the pound, would be disastrous for that monetary discipline.

Structural and Productivity Differences

He also mentions the UK's structural differences as an economy which make the assessment of the right exchange rate difficult. These are actually quite serious. He talks of oil and large foreign investment. These may require large shifts in the 'real' exchange rate, i.e. shifts in the prices of our goods relative to those of others, both measured in a common currency. Such shifts, if the nominal exchange rate is held constant, could imply unacceptable domestic inflation.

To these factors I would add productivity growth differentials. If manufacturing productivity here continues to grow at 7 per cent or so, while Germany's grows at 3 per cent, and services productivity growth is similar in our two countries at 3 per cent, this would mean that, with a constant exchange rate, even supposing it was set 'right' at the start (so as to avoid the sort of price shifts discussed in the previous paragraph), UK services inflation would be 4 per cent above German inflation. With services about two-thirds of GDP this would imply UK inflation of about 2·6 per cent above the German rate. If that rate is, say, 2 per cent, this would mean an indefinite UK inflation rate of 4·6 per cent.

This conclusion is based on the following arithmetical calculations. Suppose German inflation is 2 per cent in all sectors. Then UK manufacturers can also raise prices by 2 per cent, but with productivity growth of 7 per cent they can increase wages by 9 per cent each year. Services wages will match this, as labour will be bid into the manufacturing sector until they do, the latter sector being indefinitely expansible by international trade. But with services productivity only growing by 3 per cent, services prices will rise by 6 per cent a year. Aggregate prices will rise by 4·6 per cent = ·66 x 6 + ·34 x 2 per cent.

On the one hand, this would mean we are much closer to having an inflation rate compatible with the full EMS than the Governor seems to suggest. On the other hand, we must be quite clear that with our rapid productivity growth, zero inflation is only attainable by the UK within the EMS if German inflation is negative. This illustrates the structurally-induced strain within the EMS; it could well be resolved by having a UK rate of around 3 per cent and a zero German rate.

This is not as bad as it sounds. Sterling's purchasing power would not depreciate relative to the Deutschemark's, so it would remain totally competitive as a currency; if Germany, for example, had zero inflation, then so would Britain *in terms of EEC output in general* though not in terms of purely domestic output. All that would be happening would be that *all* currencies' purchasing power would be falling relative to UK services – or, to put it another way, UK wages would be rising in real terms faster than elsewhere in Europe. (As competition in services across EEC boundaries became a reality, we would also see a decline in the UK's production of services relative to manufactures – but that would be very long term.)

If we decide that the gains from a common money, policed by competition, exceed the gain from choosing an independent domestic inflation rate, then this is what lies ahead. It is hard to believe that the gains from the common money are not significant, whereas provided inflation is low (0-4 per cent, say), the costs may not be of any great consequence. So a reformed EMS is something that even with these structural problems we could reasonably join once our present inflationary excesses have been curbed.

Conclusions

There is plenty in the Governor's lecture with which to quibble. Regional policy is not necessary as part of EMU. Nor is fiscal co-ordination. But where it matters – on policy – the Governor's judgements are correct. EMU can be best pursued by staying with the post-Madrid control-free EMS, and allowing that to evolve – as the competitive currency system that it will be. The EMS itself is worth joining post-reform, since reform will eliminate its controls and inconsistencies. It will create strains but these are probably worth living with for the sake of the gains from having a common money, policed by competition.

The Governor has produced a memorable lecture and a constructive contribution to the debate on European monetary integration.